"Mining the ⸺ ⸺ ⸺ ⸺
intercede fo⸺ ⸺ ⸺ ⸺ ⸺ dads' greatest needs
and to consider our own duty to love and honor
them. As you seek to glorify God as the son or
daughter he's called you to be, this book will be an
excellent resource."

Megan Hill, Editor, The Gospel Coalition

"While I'm quick to pray for my husband, children,
and church, I often forget to pray for the hearts and
lives of my own parents. I'm so grateful for Chelsea's
wisdom and helpful prompts! I look forward to using
this resource in my own life."

Emily Jensen, Co-author, *Risen Motherhood*

"Chelsea Stanley equips us with biblical truth and
encouragement to pray for every kind of parent
in every kind of situation. This book is immensely
practical and has spurred me to pray faithfully and
specifically for my own parents."

Glenna Marshall, Author, *Everyday Faithfulness*

"I grew up knowing that my parents prayed for me
every day, but it took me a long time to realize I could
(and should) pray for them too. This book is a won-
derful guide to help me see how to do that in a way
that is rooted in Scripture and honoring to them."

Barnabas Piper, Author, *Hoping for Happiness*

"This book deals in things that are particularly close
to God's heart—his word, earnest prayer, and caring
for our parents. The practice Stanley invites us into
is full of promise in all seasons, both for the ones
prayed for and the one praying."

Mike Bullmore, Senior Pastor,
Crossway Community Church

"This book has blessed me so much, and has reminded me that ultimately, if I want to bless and honor my loved ones, I've got to start with prayer."
Isabel Tom, Author, *The Value of Wrinkles*

"Scripture saturated, accessible, soul-stirring, and convicting. I recommend this practical aid to young and old as a thoughtful encouragement in a duty we too easily neglect: praying for our parents. Spending time praying for your parents through this study will warm your affections, encourage repentance, and help you to implore God to do what only he can."
Greg Morse, Staff Writer, desiringGod.org

"Chelsea Stanley has blessed the church by giving us this wise and biblically sound advice on how to pray for our parents. Her model of basing our prayers directly on Scripture is both wise and instructive. Get this book and use it as a tool to bless your parents and strengthen your own prayer life."
John Dunlop M.D., Geriatrician, Author, *Finishing Well to the Glory of God*

"Chelsea Stanley gives us a necessary reminder—our parents are in need of prayer. Here's an insightful Scriptural guide to help us do just that!"
Barbara and Stacy Reaoch
(mother and daughter-in-law), Authors

"Surely one of the most important things we can do for our parents is pray for them? And yet so often we run out of steam or we're not sure how. This book will energise you and inspire you to keep going."
Matt Beeby, Rector, Saint James Gerrards Cross

THINGS TO
PRAY
5

FOR YOUR
PARENTS

CHELSEA STANLEY

thegoodbook
COMPANY

5 things to pray for your parents
Prayers that change things for an older generation
© Chelsea Stanley, 2021
Series Editor: Carl Laferton

Published by:
The Good Book Company

thegoodbook.com | thegoodbook.co.uk
thegoodbook.com.au | thegoodbook.co.nz | thegoodbook.co.in

ISBN: 9781784986285 | Printed in India

Design by André Parker

CONTENTS

PRAYING THAT I WILL...

FOREWORD

BY TIM CHALLIES

A few years ago, I wrote a series of blogs called "The Commandment We Forgot." The commandment in question was one pertaining to the whole life of every human being. It was a commandment with application to the home, church, and workplace; a commandment that provides a stable foundation to all of society. Yet it was, and is, a commandment that is sorely neglected today. It is the fifth of God's ten great commandments to humanity: "Honor your father and your mother, as the LORD your God commanded you, that your days may be long, and that it may go well with you in the land that the LORD your God is giving you" (Deuteronomy 5 v 16).

Did you notice that God attaches blessings to this commandment? Writing centuries later, the apostle Paul calls it "the first commandment with a promise" (Ephesians 6 v 2). The blessings take shape in two forms: a long life and a good life. These promises were not guarantees. Rather, they point to the truth that those who honor their parents generally experience a better life than those who do not. Why? Because those who honor their parents are doing things God's way, living in the way God created humans to live.

But what is honor? Biblically, the word honor refers to weight or significance. To honor our parents we are to attach great worth to them and great value to our relationship with them. It is to respect and revere them, to speak well of them, and to treat them with kindness, gentleness, dignity, and esteem. We are to ensure they are cared for and even to make provision for them when necessary. All of that and much more is bound up in this little word. Such honor can be expressed in a number of ways: forgiving our parents, esteeming them publicly and privately, seeking their wisdom, supporting them, and providing for them.

And here, in this little guide, Chelsea Stanley points us to another important way in which we can fulfill God's command to honor our parents: by praying for them.

To honor our parents is no easy call. We're bound to encounter difficult seasons and hard decisions. We need the Spirit's help. That's why this book is doubly useful as we seek to obey the commandment we forgot. First, as we lift our parents before the throne of grace and pray God's blessings upon them, we honor them before the Lord in that very moment. And second, as we pray for our own heart, and for our relationship with our parents, we will be empowered to love and serve them better in word and deed. And on both accounts, we can enjoy God's assurance that obeying his command to honor our parents will lead to great blessing.

Tim Challies
Blogger and Author, Challies.com

HOW TO USE THIS GUIDE

This guide will help you to pray in 21 different areas and situations for your mother or father—be they biological or adoptive, working or retired, fit or frail, married or separated, believers or unbelievers. There are five different things to pray for each of the 21 areas, so you can use this book in a variety of ways.

➤ *You can pray through a set of "five things" each day, over the course of three weeks, and then start again.*

➤ *You can take one of the prayer themes for the week and pray one point every day from Monday to Friday.*

➤ *Or you can dip in and out of it, as and when a particular need arises in your family's life.*

➤ *There's also a space on each page for you to write in the names of specific situations or concerns that you intend to remember in prayer.*

While I've used "parents" plural throughout this guide, I know that for a variety of reasons—some of them very painful—not everyone will be praying for two parents. I also acknowledge that each reader will come to this book with a unique family dynamic and history. While we can't capture everyone's particular situations in each prompt, I trust that with a bit of creativity you'll be able to consider your family's needs and adjust your prayers accordingly with the Spirit's help.

Each prayer suggestion is based on a passage of the Bible, so you can be confident as you use this guide that you are praying great prayers—prayers that God wants you to pray because they're based on his word and aligned with his heart.

As Christians, God commands us to be devoted to prayer and to honor our parents (Romans 12 v 12; Ephesians 6 v 2). When we honor our parents by including them in our prayers, we obey both commands which is doubly pleasing to God!

The command to honor our parents comes with a beautiful promise—"that it may go well with you" (Ephesians 6 v 3). I hope that you will reap this blessing as you come before God with prayers that change things for an older generation.

5 THINGS TO PRAY

PRAYING THAT GOD WILL...

SAVE MY PARENTS

JOHN 3 v 16-21

PRAYER POINTS:

_____

_____

_____

_____

Father, you are the God who saves. Please help my parents to...

KNOW GOD'S LOVE

"For God so loved the world that he gave his one and only Son" (v 16).

God's love toward our parents is deep, steadfast, and pure. Our own love for them pales in comparison. Pray that your mom and dad would look at Christ's sacrifice and know how much God loves them. Thank him for loving you with this same love too.

BELIEVE IN JESUS

"... that whoever believes in him..." (v 16).

Do your parents believe in Jesus Christ for their salvation? If they do, praise God for saving them from their sin. If they don't, pray boldly in the power of the Holy Spirit and the name of Jesus that God would cause their hearts to believe. Ask God to give you opportunities and courage to share your faith with them.

NOT PERISH

"... shall not perish..." (v 16).

Whether we're believers or not, we all have to face the fact that our earthly bodies will eventually perish. Pray that your parents would have a growing sense of their own mortality—causing them to soberly contemplate what comes after the grave and swiftly run to Jesus to escape the sting of eternal death.

 **HAVE ETERNAL LIFE**

"... but have eternal life" (v 16).

Christ died for our sins so that, if we believe in him, we might live with God and enjoy him forever in heaven. Pray that your parents would take hold of this promise and allow it to impact the way they live out the rest of their days on this earth as well.

 COME TO THE LIGHT

"But whoever lives by the truth comes into the light, so that it may be seen plainly that what they have done has been done in the sight of God" (v 21).

Those who live in the truth of the gospel—the good news that Jesus died for our sins—don't need to fear the light. What things from your parents' past or present might cause them to shrink back into the shadows? Pray that they would confidently come into the light, where sin is exposed, shame flees, and good works shine bright for God's glory.

5 THINGS TO PRAY

PRAYING THAT GOD WILL...

GIVE THEM PURPOSE

PSALM 90 v 12-17

PRAYER POINTS:

_____

_____

_____

_____

Lord, you created my parents to enjoy and glorify you. I ask you to...

HUMBLE THEM

"Teach us to number our days" (v 12).

When we "number our days," we realize that our time on earth is limited. This could have a paralyzing effect on some, but pray instead that it would propel your parents to humbly acknowledge our everlasting God and to live out the remainder of their days in his service.

HAVE COMPASSION

"Have compassion on your servants" (v 13).

How much we all need God's compassion! We belong to him, but we usurp his purpose for our lives and selfishly labor for our own success and glory instead. Take a moment to confess your own idolatry to the Lord. Then ask him to convict your parents of their sin and to have mercy on you all.

SATISFY THEIR SOULS

"Satisfy us in the morning with your unfailing love" (v 14).

The world offers our parents a smorgasbord of goodies that promise to satisfy them. They're told that *this cruise, this magic pill, this retirement village* will make them happy, but the Bible says that true satisfaction comes from God. Pray that your parents would be satisfied in him and that they would know his unfailing love day by day.

 ## SHOW YOUR DEEDS

"May your deeds be shown to your servants, your splendor to their children" (v 16).

The work of redemption is God's most marvelous deed. If your parents are God's servants, marvel at the saving work Christ accomplished on their behalf. If they are not his servants, pray that he would allow you to behold his splendor as you watch him do a work in their hearts that only he can do.

 ## ESTABLISH THEIR WORK

"Establish the work of our hands for us—yes, establish the work of our hands" (v 17).

Think about the work your parents do each day. Whether they work with their hands, sit at a desk, or volunteer in retirement, ask God to make their work fruitful—not for their own personal gain or praise, but for the good of their fellow man and the glory of God.

PRAYING THAT GOD WILL...

GRANT THEM WISDOM

PROVERBS 2 v 1-10

PRAYER POINTS:

_____

_____

_____

_____

God, you are the source of all wisdom. Make my parents wise. Please...

GIVE THEM UNDERSTANDING

"If you call out for insight and cry aloud for understanding ... then you will understand the fear of the LORD and find the knowledge of God" (v 3, 5).

God gives wisdom to those who seek it out. Pray that your parents wouldn't rely on their own insight or the insight of others but would instead call out to the Lord for wisdom grounded in the fear of him.

SPEAK THROUGH YOUR WORD

"The LORD gives wisdom; from his mouth come knowledge and understanding" (v 6).

Praise God for making himself known and speaking to us through his word. Ask him to give your parents wisdom as they read the Scriptures. Pray that they would have open ears and humble hearts that are ready to receive knowledge and understanding.

PROTECT THEM

"For he guards the course of the just and protects the way of his faithful ones" (v 8).

God offers his protection to those who belong to him. If your parents have not entrusted themselves to his care, pray that they would put their faith in Jesus. If they are already among the faithful, ask God to protect them from temptation, sin, and the attacks of the evil one as they walk in wisdom.

 ## LEAD THEM

"Then you will understand what is right and just and fair—every good path" (v 9).

Pray that your parents wouldn't try to blaze their own trail, but would instead walk on the good path laid by God. Think of specific situations and decisions your parents are facing today and ask God to lead them where he wants them to go.

 ## PUT WISDOM IN THEIR HEARTS

"For wisdom will enter your heart, and knowledge will be pleasant to your soul" (v 10).

Pray that your mom and dad would delight in the way of wisdom and acquire a taste for its sweet fruit. If you already see this fruit in their lives, bless the Spirit for putting wisdom into their hearts. Pray that you would receive your parents' wisdom with a teachable spirit and a grateful heart.

5 THINGS TO PRAY

PRAYING THAT GOD WILL...

BLESS THEIR RELATIONSHIPS

PROVERBS

PRAYER POINTS:

_____

_____

_____

_____

Father, please bless my parents through their relationships, especially with their...

 SPOUSE

> *"He who finds a wife finds what is good and receives favor from the LORD" (18 v 22).*

Marriage is a kindness from God intended to bless us. If your parents are married (or remarried), pray that he would show them his favor by strengthening their love for each other and for Christ. Ask the one who joined them together to protect their marriage against sin, complacency, and Satan's schemes.

 CHILDREN

> *"The father of a righteous child has great joy; a man who fathers a wise son rejoices in him" (23 v 24).*

This verse tells us that we can be instruments of God's blessing toward our parents—what a privilege! Pray today that you and any siblings you have would bring joy to your mother and father by doing what's right in God's eyes.

GRANDKIDS

"Children's children are a crown to the aged, and parents are the pride of their children" (17 v 6).

God loves the generations—they're part of his good design for families. If your parents are grandparents, pray that they would treasure their grandchildren and find great joy in those special relationships. Whether or not they're grandparents, ask God to use your parents to proclaim his works to the next generation.

FRIENDS

"A friend loves at all times" (17 v 17).

Ask the Lord to provide your parents with godly friends who will faithfully encourage and exhort them in truth and love. Thank him for the friends they already have, and pray for them by name. Pray that your parents would be good friends to others too—loving them well and building them up.

CHURCH

"As iron sharpens iron, so one person sharpens another" (27 v 17).

Sanctification doesn't happen in a bubble. Pray that God would use your parents' church family to sharpen their faith, and that your mom and dad would, in turn, help younger believers grow in maturity. If your parents aren't Christians, pray that the church's witness might play a role in winning them to Christ.

THINGS TO
PRAY
5

PRAYING THAT GOD WILL...

BRING
THEM JOY

PSALM 16 v 8-11

PRAYER POINTS:

_____

_____

_____

_____

God, true happiness comes from you. Grant my parents...

 UNSHAKEABLE HOPE

> *"I keep my eyes always on the LORD. With him at my right hand, I will not be shaken"* (v 8).

In a world filled with constant distractions, pray that your parents would keep their eyes on the Lord and place their hope firmly in Christ, who fills us with all joy. Pray that whatever sorrows or trials may come in the future—or already cloud the present—your parents would not be shaken, because God is with them.

 A GLAD HEART

> *"Therefore my heart is glad and my tongue rejoices"* (v 9).

David, the writer of this psalm, was satisfied in the Lord, calling him "my portion and my cup" (v 5). "Therefore," he sang, "my heart is glad." Pray that your parents, like David, would rejoice in God and delight in his presence and provision.

SECURITY

> *"My body also will rest secure, because you will not abandon me to the realm of the dead" (v 9-10).*

So often it's fear that robs our joy. Your mom and dad may look to financial advisors, doctors, government programs, or family for security. While these people and services can offer some peace of mind, pray that your parents would find their ultimate security in the death and resurrection of Jesus Christ.

 ## TRUE LIFE

> *"You make known to me the path of life" (v 11).*

Pray that God would show your parents the path of life. We can't find this path on our own. We need God to make it known to us through Jesus, who is himself "the way and the truth and the life" (John 14 v 6).

 ## ETERNAL PLEASURES

> *"You will fill me with joy in your presence, with eternal pleasures at your right hand" (v 11).*

Jesus is the King who will sit at the right hand of the Father forever, experiencing the full joy of heaven with the people he redeemed. Pray that, more and more, your parents would eagerly anticipate the eternal pleasures awaiting those who follow Christ— and that this would give them joy today.

PRAYING THAT MY PARENTS WILL...

DELIGHT IN GOD'S WORD

PSALM 119 v 12-16

PRAYER POINTS:

_____

_____

_____

_____

O Lord, I want my parents to taste the goodness of your word. May they...

PRAISE YOU

"Praise be to you, LORD; teach me your decrees" (v 12).

Pray that your parents would open the Bible and burst into praise as they read about who God is and what he's done. Bless the Lord for giving us his inspired written word.

SPEAK YOUR WORD

"With my lips I recount all the laws that come from your mouth" (v 13).

Who is within earshot of your parents? Grandkids? Co-workers? Neighbors? Caregivers? Friends? Sunday School students? Pray that your parents would use their lips to share what they've learned from God's word with anyone who will listen. If your parents aren't Christians, pray that God would give them ears to hear the gospel preached from someone else's lips.

REJOICE IN OBEDIENCE

> *"I rejoice in following your statutes as one rejoices in great riches" (v 14).*

Choosing God's way isn't always easy, but obedience to his word yields eternal rewards. Pray that your parents would obey God with joyful hearts and that he would richly bless them as they put what they read into action.

 ## MEDITATE ON YOUR PRECEPTS

> *"I meditate on your precepts and consider your ways" (v 15).*

Depending on their stage of life, your parents might find themselves with more time and space to meditate on God's word or, conversely, with a reduced ability for memorization and recall. Ask the Spirit to help your parents hide God's word in their hearts and to bring passages to mind throughout their day. Pray that their meditation would lead them to praise God, confess sin, pursue holiness, and give thanks to the Lord.

 ## READ AND DELIGHT

> *"I delight in your decrees; I will not neglect your word" (v 16).*

God's word is a feast for hungry souls, and he invites us to partake of it daily. Pray that your parents would crave God's word each morning, read it, and delight in what it says. Ask God to remove any distractions that might cause your parents to neglect his word.

PRAYING THAT MY PARENTS WILL...

LOVE GOD
AND OTHERS

MARK 12 v 30-31

PRAYER POINTS:

_____

_____

_____

_____

God, I pray that my mom and dad would love you with all their...

HEART

> *"Love the Lord your God with all your heart" (v 30).*

Our hearts toward God can grow cold and calloused over time if we're not vigilant. Pray that the Lord would stir your parents' affections and warm their hearts toward him. If they don't love God, pray that he would give them new hearts and put a new spirit within them (Ezekiel 36 v 26).

SOUL

> *"... and with all your soul" (v 30).*

God created us to love him with all that we are—our distinct personalities, passions, emotions, thoughts, humor, and dispositions. Take a moment to think about how God made your parents. Thank him for creating your mom and dad as unique image-bearers with eternal souls and pray that they would love God with their entire beings.

MIND

"... and with all your mind" (v 30).

The more we learn about God, the more we realize how much we still have left to learn. Pray that your parents would be life-long learners who actively study God's word and seek to know him better. Pray that this knowledge would lead to a deeper love for their Savior.

 ## STRENGTH

"... and with all your strength" (v 30).

As you look to the years ahead, pray that your parents would use every last ounce of strength to love and glorify God—bowing their grey-haired heads in reverence and lifting their wrinkled hands in praise. Pray that they would use everything in their power—including their skills and resources—to demonstrate their love for him as well.

 ## ... AND LOVE THEIR NEIGHBORS

"Love your neighbor as yourself" (v 31).

Think about the specific people your mom and dad come in regular contact with. Pray that your parents would demonstrate their love for God by loving these people and seeking their good. If your parents don't know Christ's love yet, ask God to soften their hearts and enable them to receive it; then pray that they would be motivated to love others because of Christ's love for them.

PRAYING THAT MY PARENTS WILL...

NOT BE ANXIOUS

PHILIPPIANS 4 v 4-9

PRAYER POINTS:

_____

_____

_____

_____

Father, when anxiety creeps in, please help my parents to...

REJOICE IN THE LORD

"Rejoice in the Lord always. I will say it again: Rejoice!" (v 4).

What life circumstances might be tempting your parents toward anxiety? It's easy to get consumed with the worries of this world, so Paul reminds us—not once, but twice—to rejoice in the Lord. Pray that in the midst of hard things, your parents would have a deep joy in our God who never changes or fails.

KNOW THE LORD IS NEAR

"The Lord is near" (v 5).

Sometimes we worry for our parents. Praise the Lord for being near to you and for watching over them—even when you can't. Pray that these sweet assurances would help you trust your heavenly Father to care for your mom and dad. Spend time now talking to God about specific things that are worrying you or them, knowing that he hears you.

PRAY

> *"Do not be anxious about anything, but in every situation, by prayer and petition, with thanksgiving, present your requests to God" (v 6).*

Where do your parents tend to turn in anxious moments? Perhaps they turn outwards toward comforts like friends, food, social media, or alcohol. Maybe they turn inwards in self-reliance. Pray that they would instead turn upwards toward God in prayer.

 BE AT PEACE

> *"And the peace of God, which transcends all understanding, will guard your hearts and your minds in Christ Jesus" (v 7).*

Ask God to grant your parents his perfect peace and to guard their hearts and minds from anxiety in Christ Jesus. If your parents aren't followers of Jesus, pray that they would see the peace of God within you and desire it for themselves.

 THINK ON CHRIST

> *"Whatever is true ... noble ... right ... pure ... lovely ... admirable ... think about such things" (v 8).*

Anxious minds can spiral quickly. Pray that your parents would immediately reject anxious thoughts and instead think on Christ, our most "excellent" and "praiseworthy" Savior (v 8), so that anxiety gains no foothold in their hearts.

THINGS TO
PRAY
5

PRAYING THAT MY PARENTS WILL...

BE CONTENT

1 TIMOTHY 6 v 6-12

PRAYER POINTS:

_____

_____

_____

_____

Lord God, giver of all things good, may my parents…

 BE GRATEFUL

> *"Godliness with contentment is great gain"*
> *(v 6).*

Are your parents discontent with their circumstances? Maybe they wish they lived closer to family or they can't wait to retire. Perhaps their bodies are failing them or they resent needing help. Pray that instead of being consumed by what they don't have, they would be grateful for what God has already given them—especially the gift of his Son.

 THINK ETERNALLY

> *"For we brought nothing into the world, and we can take nothing out of it" (v 7).*

Stock prices plummet, china breaks, and silver tarnishes. Pray that your parents wouldn't chase after perishable riches, but would instead anticipate their heavenly inheritance which has been secured by Christ. If they don't know Jesus, pray that they would be dissatisfied with what the world has to offer and find lasting contentment in Christ.

TRUST IN GOD'S PROVISION

"But if we have food and clothing, we will be content with that" (v 8).

As they age, your parents may feel less in control of their finances, health, or even their own personal care. Pray that this feeling would not lead them to fear or despair, but to a contented trust that God will supply their daily needs. Humbly ask God how he might want to use you to provide for some of these needs.

 ## AVOID TEMPTATION

"Those who want to get rich fall into temptation" (v 9).

Discontentment and the love of money may tempt us to hoard, cheat, grumble, or envy. Pray that your parents would not fall into these traps, but would walk closely with God who protects us from the snares of sin.

 ## PURSUE RIGHTEOUSNESS

"Pursue righteousness, godliness, faith, love, endurance and gentleness" (v 11).

Outside voices tell our parents to pursue a life of comfort and ease, but God wants them to pursue righteousness. Pray that your parents would joyfully submit themselves to God's ways and look to Christ as their example and strength.

THINGS TO PRAY

5

PRAYING THAT MY PARENTS WILL...

ENDURE

HEBREWS 12 v 1-12

PRAYER POINTS:

_____

_____

_____

_____

Father, as my parents get closer to the finish line, grant them endurance. Help them to...

RUN WITH PERSEVERANCE

"Let us throw off everything that hinders ... and let us run with perseverance the race marked out for us" (v 1).

Pray that your parents would lay aside sin, distractions, or anything else that might weigh them down so that they can run the final laps of the race marked out for them by God with gusto! If they're not believers, pray that God would graciously lead them to the starting line.

CONSIDER JESUS

"... fixing our eyes on Jesus, the pioneer and perfecter of faith" (v 2).

Pray that your parents would fix their eyes on Jesus—the one who has already conquered death and is cheering us on as we run toward him. Pray that with each passing year, they would treasure Christ more dearly—or that they might truly see and embrace Jesus for the very first time.

ACCEPT DISCIPLINE

"Endure hardship as discipline; God is treating you as his children" (v 7).

It might feel a little backwards to ask God to discipline your parents. But if we believe that God disciplines his children out of love, then we should gladly ask him to discipline both them and us so that we "may share in his holiness" (v 10). Take a moment to do that now.

 LOOK TO THE HARVEST

"It produces a harvest of righteousness and peace for those who have been trained by it" (v 11).

Pray that God would use the trials your parents are facing right now to produce good fruit in them—making them more steadfast, more perfect, and more complete as they practice trusting him. Ask God to help your parents see beyond the immediate pain of discipline and look to the harvest of righteousness and peace they will one day reap.

 BE STRONG

"Therefore, strengthen your feeble arms and weak knees" (v 12).

Thank God for all the people he has used over the years to strengthen your faith and help you endure—your spiritual fathers and mothers. Take time to pray for them too, asking God to grant them stamina as they seek to serve him.

THINGS TO
5
PRAY

PRAYING WHEN MY PARENTS ARE...

MAKING TRANSITIONS

DEUTERONOMY 31 v 6-8

PRAYER POINTS:

_____

_____

_____

_____

God, as the Israelites began a new journey in a new place under a new leader, you remained the same. And you still do! Be a constant for my parents in their...

 ## RETIREMENT

> *"Be strong and courageous. Do not be afraid or terrified because of them, for the LORD your God goes with you"* (v 6).

Retirement can be such an exciting time, but it can also come with uncertainty. Thank God for your parents' work, and pray that they would face their retirement years with courage, knowing that God will go with them. If your parents don't know God as their Lord, ask him to save them so that they might spend their retirement proclaiming his name to the world.

 ## EMPTY NESTING

> *"He will never leave you nor forsake you"* (v 6).

It's natural for parents to feel sad when their kids leave the nest. Praise God for his steadfast love, and pray that your parents will look to him to fill the void they might feel in your absence.

 **MOVING**

"The LORD himself goes before you" (v 8).

In this season of life, your parents may need to downsize, relocate, or move into a long-term care facility. Moving can be stressful and emotionally taxing—for our parents and for us—but we can take heart knowing that our LORD goes before us. Pray that you and your parents would trust God to provide grace for the future, wherever that may be.

 GRIEF

"… and will be with you" (v 8).

As our parents get older, they will likely become more and more acquainted with grief. Pray that God will be near to them as they mourn the deaths of friends and family and that they will find comfort in his presence.

 OTHER TRANSITIONS

"Do not be afraid; do not be discouraged" (v 8).

Take a moment to think about the transitions that your parents are currently facing. Ask God to reveal how he might want you to encourage them during this time. Pray that whatever transitions may come, your parents would face them without fear.

PRAYING WHEN MY PARENTS ARE...

SUFFERING

PSALM 103 v 1-14

PRAYER POINTS:

_____

_____

_____

_____

Lord, help my parents to bless your name and re-member your benefits as they face…

 ## SICKNESS

"… who forgives all your sins and heals all your diseases" (v 3).

God understands how hard it is to watch a loved one suffer from illness or pain. While we know from the big picture of Scripture that God doesn't always heal our diseases this side of heaven, he still instructs us to pray in faith for the sick (James 5 v 14). Ask him to heal your parents and to make their souls well in Christ.

 ## FINANCIAL HARDSHIP

"… and crowns you with love and compassion, who satisfies your desires with good things" (v 4-5).

Your parents might be suffering under the weight of mounting medical bills, dwindling savings, bad investments, or unemployment. Pray that the Lord would provide for their daily needs with good things and that they would know the riches of Christ's love for them.

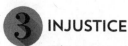

3 INJUSTICE

*"The LORD works righteousness and justice
for all the oppressed" (v 6).*

Injustice against aging image-bearers grieves the heart
of God, and it should grieve our hearts too. Perhaps
your parents have been slandered, disrespected, or
even fallen prey to abuse or fraud. Pray that God would
execute justice on their behalf and that they (and you)
would trust him in the meantime.

4 RELATIONAL STRIFE

*"The LORD is compassionate and gracious,
slow to anger, abounding in love" (v 8).*

Friends and family will sometimes fail each other, but
the Lord is *always* compassionate and gracious, slow
to anger, and abounding in love. If your parents are
suffering from relational heartache, or if your own
relationship with them is strained, ask God to restore
these relationships and to help you all treat others in
a way that reflects his character.

5 CONSEQUENCES OF SIN

*"He does not treat us as our sins deserve or
repay us according to our iniquities" (v 10).*

God may allow us to experience the consequences of
our sin, and yet he is kind to spare his children from
what we most deserve. If your parents are feeling the
sting of their own sin right now, ask God to use their
suffering to make them turn to Christ for mercy.

PRAYING WHEN MY PARENTS ARE...

LONELY

PSALM 25 v 14-18

PRAYER POINTS:

_____

_____

_____

_____

Heavenly Father, when my parents feel alone, please grant them...

FRIENDSHIP

"The LORD confides in those who fear him" (v 14).

Why might your parents be feeling lonely? Perhaps they're far from loved ones, living alone, sick in a hospital bed, missing old friends, estranged from family, or unable to keep up with conversations like they used to. Pray that God would be a faithful friend to them in the midst of their loneliness.

GRACE

"Turn to me and be gracious to me" (v 16).

People may turn away from us, but God graciously turns toward his children. Pray that your mom and dad would grasp the depth of God's love toward them and receive it with grateful hearts. Thank him for being gracious to you too.

 **COMFORT**

"For I am lonely and afflicted" (v 16).

David first spoke these words, but they were fulfilled in King Jesus who was despised and rejected by the very people he came to save. Pray that your parents would find comfort in Christ and draw near to God through him. Ask your heavenly Father to reveal how you might also be a comfort to your parents in their loneliness; pray for strength to love them well.

 RELIEF

"Relieve the troubles of my heart and free me from my anguish" (v 17).

Loneliness can take a toll on our hearts and minds—causing us to believe Satan's lies or doubt God's love for us. Pray that God would free your parents from any anxiety or anguish they may be experiencing and that they would cast their cares upon the Lord.

 MERCY

"Look on my affliction and my distress and take away all my sins" (v 18).

Sometimes we bring isolation upon ourselves through the choices we make. Pray that the Spirit would convict your parents of any sinful patterns that may be contributing to their loneliness and prompt them to seek forgiveness from God and others. If your parents have sinned toward you, ask God to give you a posture of humility and mercy toward them so that you're ready to forgive as Christ has forgiven you.

THINGS TO PRAY 5

PRAYING WHEN MY PARENTS ARE...

CARING FOR LOVED ONES

EPHESIANS 4 v 29-32

PRAYER POINTS:

_____

_____

_____

_____

Father, care for my parents as they care for the ones they love. Help them to...

 SPEAK GRACIOUS WORDS

"Do not let any unwholesome talk come out of your mouths, but only what is helpful for building others up according to their needs" (v 29).

If your parents are caring for a loved one right now—maybe an aging parent, a child with special needs, or a sick spouse—ask God to help them as they do the good and God-honoring task before them. Pray that your parents would encourage the ones they're caring for—never tearing them down in frustration or impatience, but speaking gracious words that build up.

 PUT AWAY BITTERNESS

"Get rid of all bitterness" (v 31).

Tending to the needs of a loved one can be mentally, emotionally, and physically draining at times. Pray that your parents would not allow bitterness to take hold of their hearts but would serve others with joy.

BE KIND

"Be kind" (v 32).

Our heavenly Father is so kind to care for us. Praise him for being such a good and generous King! Pray that your parents would imitate Christ's kindness toward us by sacrificially loving those in need. Ask God to bless your parents with life, righteousness, and honor as they selflessly give of their time, resources, and energy (Proverbs 21 v 21).

HAVE COMPASSION

"... and compassionate to one another" (v 32).

It can be difficult for once fully capable people to receive help. Pray that your parents would be understanding and compassionate toward the ones they're caring for, even when their efforts aren't recognized or appreciated.

FORGIVE OTHERS

"Forgiving each other, just as in Christ God forgave you" (v 32).

Caregiving requires a certain amount of trust for both parties involved. When that trust is broken, it can put a real strain on the relationship. Pray that your parents and the ones they're caring for would overlook minor offenses and be quick to forgive each other if there's a breach of trust. Thank God for always being trustworthy and for forgiving us in Christ.

THINGS TO
PRAY

PRAYING WHEN MY PARENTS ARE...

LOSING THEIR MEMORY

PSALM 102

PRAYER POINTS:

_____

_____

_____

_____

Lord, my parents can't remember like they used to.
As I walk alongside them, I ask you to...

HEAR MY CRY

"Hear my prayer, LORD; let my cry for help
come to you" (v 1).

Caring for a parent suffering from memory loss can
be excruciating. Take some time to cry out to your
heavenly Father today and sit with him in your grief.
Share your fears, frustrations, and heartache with the
one who hears our prayers.

ANSWER ME

"Turn your ear to me; when I call, answer
me quickly" (v 2).

Call to God for wisdom and help as you navigate
your parent's cognitive decline. Ask him to grant you
strength, endurance, patience, hope, and love as you
care for your parents. Perhaps you feel bad that you're
not doing enough, or that you need to seek outside
care—ask God to free you from shame and guilt and
help you to see yourself, and your situation, as he sees
you in Christ.

HAVE PITY ON THEM

> *"My heart is blighted and withered like grass; I forget to eat my food. In my distress I groan aloud" (v 4-5).*

It's heart-wrenching to watch someone you love grow increasingly afraid, paranoid, angry, or confused. Ask the Lord to quiet your mom or dad's heart and give them moments of peace. Pray that he would have pity on them and protect them from harm.

HELP US PRAISE YOU

> *"The name of the LORD will be declared in Zion and his praise in Jerusalem" (v 21).*

If your parents are Christians, dementia will not have the final word. Rejoice that you and your parents will one day praise God together in the heavenly Jerusalem with restored minds and bodies. If they are not yet believers, ask God to reach where you can't—into their souls—and cause them to call on the name of Jesus.

HELP US REMEMBER

> *"But you remain the same" (v 27).*

When your parents change, God remains the same. When they can't remember your name, he remembers yours *and* theirs. What hope we have in him! Take hold of these truths today and ask the Lord to bring them to mind on your hardest days. Pray that God would give your parents clear and precious glimpses of himself amidst the darkness and that he would be with them in the hidden places of their hearts.

5 THINGS TO PRAY

PRAYING WHEN MY PARENTS ARE...

FACING DEATH

2 CORINTHIANS 5 v 1-10

PRAYER POINTS:

_____

_____

_____

_____

God, as my parents anticipate their death, may they…

LONG FOR HEAVEN

"Meanwhile we groan, longing to be clothed instead with our heavenly dwelling" (v 2).

As your parents contemplate their declining strength and health, pray that God would loosen their hearts' grip on this world and make them long for heaven. Thank God for the time he's given you with your mom and dad, and ask him to help you cling to Christ more tightly than you cling to your parents.

BE CONFIDENT

"We are always confident and know that as long as we are at home in the body we are away from the Lord" (v 6).

Ask God to give your parents confidence in the face of death and the courage that only comes from holding to Christ's resurrection. If they are not Christians, ask God to open their eyes to the truth and put gospel courage into their hearts before they die.

LIVE BY FAITH

"For we live by faith, not by sight" (v 7).

Looking back on their lives, your parents might regret missed opportunities, doubt God's goodness, or feel ashamed of their sin. Call upon God to bolster their faith so that they might have full assurance of Christ's forgiveness and love toward them in their final days.

 ## AIM TO PLEASE GOD

"So we make it our goal to please him" (v 9).

Pray that your parents would submit both their lives and deaths as humble offerings to God. Pray that they would be intentional with their remaining money, time, gifts, words, and talents—faithfully stewarding every last bit in a way that serves God and others.

 ## SERVE CHRIST

"For we must all appear before the judgment seat of Christ, so that each of us may receive what is due us for the things done while in the body, whether good or bad" (v 10).

After we die, we will stand before Christ, our righteous Judge. Our deeds don't save us, but they're indicators of our faith in Jesus. Pray that your parents would live in faithful obedience now so that Christ might one day say, "Well done, good and faithful servant … Come and share your master's happiness" (Matthew 25 v 21).

PRAYING THAT I WILL...

TRUST GOD AS MY FATHER

EPHESIANS 3 v 14-21

PRAYER POINTS:

_____

_____

_____

_____

Father, I am first and foremost your child. Please help me to remember these truths...

YOU HAVE A PLAN FOR ME

"For this reason I kneel before the Father, from whom every family in heaven and on earth derives its name" (v 14-15).

Bow before your Father, acknowledging him as the one who has named every family in heaven and on earth—even yours! Praise him for adopting you as his child and for placing you into your earthly family as part of his good plan. If you struggle to understand his plan, ask God to give you eyes to see his goodness and faith to trust his character.

YOU WILL STRENGTHEN ME

"I pray that out of his glorious riches he may strengthen you with power through his Spirit in your inner being" (v 16).

Where do you feel weak as a son or daughter? Pray that your Father would strengthen you with his power and give you unwavering faith in Jesus Christ.

YOU LOVE ME

"And I pray that you, being rooted and established in love, may have power ... to grasp how wide and long and high and deep is the love of Christ" (v 17b-18).

God designed the parent-child relationship to give us glimpses of his love for us; however, sometimes our parents don't love us the way God intended. If their love is lacking, ask God to help you grasp Christ's perfect, unfailing, lavish love toward you today, and praise him for it.

 ## YOU ARE ABLE

"To him who is able to do immeasurably more than all we ask or imagine..." (v 20).

Are there any prayer requests you have for your parents that seem impossible right now? Maybe you've been earnestly praying for their salvation or pleading with God for relational healing. Bring these requests before your Father with renewed confidence, trusting that he is able to do far more abundantly than all we ask or think!

 ## YOU ARE WORTHY

"To him be glory in the church and in Christ Jesus throughout all generations, for ever and ever!" (v 21).

Lift your hands and give God glory! Pray that he will continue to be glorified in your family for many generations to come.

5 THINGS TO PRAY

PRAYING THAT I WILL...

GIVE THANKS

PSALM 100

PRAYER POINTS:

_____

_____

_____

_____

I will give thanks to you, O Lord, for you are...

OUR MAKER

"Know that the LORD is God. It is he who made us, and we are his" (v 3).

God took such care in creating you—ordaining each of your days and intricately knitting you together in your mother's womb (Psalm 139 v 13-16). Give thanks for the man and woman he brought together to give you life. Thank him not only for making you but for making you *his*.

OUR SHEPHERD

"We are his people, the sheep of his pasture" (v 3).

Jesus is a good shepherd. Thank him for calling you by name and for willingly laying down his life for you, his sheep. Reflect on how he has led you, protected you, restored you, and comforted you throughout your life—sometimes by way of your mother and father—and give thanks.

GOOD

"For the Lord is good" (v 5).

We have a good Father who gives us good gifts. Bless him for generously pouring out his grace and mercy on you through his son, Jesus Christ. Thank him for blessing you with adoption, redemption, forgiveness, and a guaranteed inheritance. In addition to these spiritual blessings, express your gratitude for the good gifts he has given you by the hands of your parents as well; thank him for a few specifically.

STEADFAST IN LOVE

"His love endures forever" (v 5).

When human love waivers, God's love endures. Thank him for loving you so much that he has called you his child and for promising never to let anyone snatch you out of his hand (John 10 v 29).

FAITHFUL

"His faithfulness continues through all generations" (v 5).

The Lord has been faithful to your parents' generation, he is faithful to your generation, and he will continue to be faithful to future generations. Thanks be to God! Take a moment to recall specific instances of God's faithfulness toward you and your family. Then as the psalmist writes, "Shout for joy to the Lord ... Worship the Lord with gladness; come before him with joyful songs" (v 1-2).

5 THINGS TO PRAY

PRAYING THAT I WILL...

LOVE MY PARENTS

ROMANS 12 v 9-21

PRAYER POINTS:

_____

_____

_____

_____

God, I want to love my parents well. Supply the grace I need to...

HONOR

> *"Honor one another above yourselves"*
> *(v 10).*

In the Old Testament, the word honor means to "give weight." Ask God to help you honor your parents by giving them the proper weight in your heart and life. Pray that you would reflect our merciful Savior, who honored us by seating us in the heavenly places with Christ, despite our sinful state (Ephesians 2 v 5-6).

PRAY

> *"Be joyful in hope, patient in affliction,*
> *faithful in prayer" (v 12).*

You're in a position to be one of your parents' biggest prayer advocates. Ask God to help you love your parents by continuing to intercede for them before the throne of grace. In what particular areas do your parents need your faithful prayer? Bring those requests before God now, and praise him for hearing you.

 ### WELCOME

"Practice hospitality" (v 13).

Thank God for welcoming you into his family and inviting you to sit at his table. Ask him to show you ways in which you can welcome your parents into your home and life. Pray that you would be willing to sacrifice your time, resources, and comfort out of love for God and your parents.

 ### BLESS

"Bless those who persecute you; bless and do not curse" (v 14).

Whether you have a great relationship with your parents or a troubled one, pray God's blessing upon them. Ask the Lord to make his face shine upon them and to grant them grace and peace. Thank God for your parents—and for the other parental figures in your life—recalling specific ways God has used this generation to minister to you.

 ### LIVE AT PEACE

"If it is possible, as far as it depends on you, live at peace with everyone" (v 18).

As Christians, we're called to follow Christ's example by living at peace with everyone—including family!— as far as it depends on us. Thankfully, we don't have to muster up peace in our own strength. The Prince of Peace equips us to make peace with others. Ask him to grant you peace today.

PRAYING THAT I WILL...

SEEK FORGIVENESS

1 CORINTHIANS 13 v 4-7

PRAYER POINTS:

_____

_____

_____

_____

Father, I desire to love my parents how Christ has loved me. Please forgive me for the times I have been...

 IMPATIENT

"Love is patient" (v 4).

Sometimes it's hard to be patient with your parents. Maybe they're forgetful or slow-moving. Perhaps they hold to different political beliefs or parenting philosophies. If you've been impatient with your parents, turn away from your sin and turn toward your Father who is endlessly patient with you. Ask him to help you joyfully bear with your parents, even when it's hard.

 UNKIND

"Love is kind" (v 4).

Are you ever rude to your parents? Perhaps you've belittled them, interrupted them, poked fun at them, or been sarcastic toward them. Repent of your unkind attitude and speech and ask God to help you be more like Christ—showering your parents with words of kindness.

PROUD

"It is not proud" (v 4).

In our pride, we sometimes think we know better than our parents and may dismiss them as old-fashioned or out of touch. Ask God to reveal any pride that may reside in your heart and confess it to him. Pray for increasing humility as you count your parents as more significant than yourself (Philippians 2 v 3).

SELF-SEEKING

"It is not self-seeking" (v 5). .

Have you ever treated your parents like a vending machine—expecting them to give you whatever you want whenever you ask for it? Although it's right for our parents to delight in giving their children good gifts, we must guard ourselves against selfishly taking advantage of their kindness. Thank God for the ways your parents have served you and repent of the times you've been entitled or ungrateful.

UNFORGIVING

"It keeps no record of wrongs" (v 5).

Parents may be some of the most difficult people to forgive. After all, we expect them to nurture and protect us, not cause us pain. If your parents have sinned against you, pray that God would help you to be willing to forgive them. Confess any bitterness you have toward them and entrust your pain to Christ. He will mercifully carry your heavy burdens and graciously exchange them for a lighter load (Matthew 11 v 28-30).

PRAYING THAT I WILL...

CARE FOR
MY PARENTS

PHILIPPIANS 2 v 1-8

PRAYER POINTS:

_____

_____

_____

_____

God, I am grateful that you care for me. As I care for my parents, please help me to…

 ## BE ENCOURAGED

"Therefore if you have any encouragement from being united with Christ…" (v 1).

How encouraging it is to know that we are united with Christ! If you're feeling discouraged as you care for an aging or sick parent, remember your connection with Jesus in whom you have redemption, security, and grace. You are not in this alone—he is with you every step of the way.

 ## BE COMFORTED BY LOVE

"… if any comfort from his love…" (v 1).

Transitioning into the role of caregiver can be painful—especially when you're caring for a person who cared for you for so long. Bare your heart to God today and let him comfort you with his love.

BE HUMBLE

> *"Do nothing out of selfish ambition or vain conceit. Rather, in humility value others above yourselves" (v 3).*

Honoring your parents may become increasingly difficult as you become a sort of authority over them. You may have to give them instructions and make decisions on their behalf. Pray that you would be humble, gracious, and kind as you do these things.

 SEE THEIR NEEDS

> *"… not looking to your own interests but each of you to the interests of the others" (v 4).*

Ask the Holy Spirit to help you see your parents' needs. Pray for wisdom as you make the hard decisions that come along with caregiving. Surrender your own interests or preferences to God and ask him to show you what is in the best interests of your parents.

 IMITATE CHRIST

> *"In your relationships with one another, have the same mindset as Christ" (v 5).*

Even though Jesus is God, "he made himself nothing by taking the very nature of a servant … he humbled himself by becoming obedient to death—even death on a cross!" (v 6-8). Pray that God would help you imitate Christ, giving you a heart that is eager to obey God and serve your parents. Praise the Lord Jesus for being the perfect example of humility.

EXPLORE THE WHOLE SERIES

thegoodbook
COMPANY

BIBLICAL | RELEVANT | ACCESSIBLE

At The Good Book Company, we are dedicated to helping Christians and local churches grow. We believe that God's growth process always starts with hearing clearly what he has said to us through his timeless word—the Bible.

Ever since we opened our doors in 1991, we have been striving to produce Bible-based resources that bring glory to God. We have grown to become an international provider of user-friendly resources to the Christian community, with believers of all backgrounds and denominations using our books, Bible studies, devotionals, evangelistic resources, and DVD-based courses.

We want to equip ordinary Christians to live for Christ day by day, and churches to grow in their knowledge of God, their love for one another, and the effectiveness of their outreach.

Call us for a discussion of your needs or visit one of our local websites for more information on the resources and services we provide.

Your friends at The Good Book Company

thegoodbook.com | thegoodbook.co.uk
thegoodbook.com.au | thegoodbook.co.nz
thegoodbook.co.in